Funmilayo Adesanya-Davies

CORONAVIRUS

Funmilayo Adesanya-Davies

CORONAVIRUS

An Anthology V-I

JustFiction Edition

Imprint

Any brand names and product names mentioned in this book are subject to trademark, brand or patent protection and are trademarks or registered trademarks of their respective holders. The use of brand names, product names, common names, trade names, product descriptions etc. even without a particular marking in this work is in no way to be construed to mean that such names may be regarded as unrestricted in respect of trademark and brand protection legislation and could thus be used by anyone.

Cover image: www.ingimage.com

Publisher:
JustFiction! Edition
is a trademark of
International Book Market Service Ltd., member of OmniScriptum Publishing Group
17 Meldrum Street, Beau Bassin 71504, Mauritius
Printed at: see last page
ISBN: 978-620-0-49073-5

CORONAVIRUS
An Anthology

V-I

By

'Funmilayo Adesanya-Davies Ph.D

Department of English and Communication Arts

Faculty of Humanities

Ignatius Ajuru University of Education

Port Harcourt, Rivers State, Nigeria

Email: mercyfunmi5@gmail.com

+234(0)8057142287

Dedicated to the Almighty God and all whose words inspired me

Table of Contents

FOREWORD

It is no more news that the Coronavirus has ravaged the whole world and this has crippled the global economic activities of both developed and developing countries of the world. Since been recorded last year in China, the COVID-19 has been declared a pandemic by the World Health Organization (WHO). Scores of dead bodies are littered on streets, sending countries into lockdown as health service providers struggles to provide medical assistance to citizens.

It is of great importance for countries to strive to carry out precautionary measures to curtail and make the PANDEMIC to die a natural death. Thus, the core aim of Prof. Ade-Davies International Foundation (PMADIF) towards this PANDEMIC era is to ensure that we discover cure and vaccines which can help stop the spread of this disease virus.

PMADIF which is non-profit organization is a community of active citizens that works to ensure that human life is protected with dignity; the human specie existence is not threatened and our freedoms are respected worldwide, among other goals. PMADIF members live in every nation of the world. Our team is Nigeria based but has a wide spread across Nigeria, Africa and other parts of the world.

All the countries and individuals in the world are trying their best in the fight against the Coronavirus. Prof. Funmilayo Adesanya-Davies is the founder and Chairman Board of PMADIF. Her poetic thoughts in this book is additionally part of her contribution to the lessons, loss, gain and recovering process of the COVID-19 pandemic saga of 2019/2020. She wrote her narrative poems as a linguist, didactic in her approach in the entertaining and teaching process, as she intended to teach people something, especially moral lessons.

Funmilayo Adesanya-Davies narrative poems in this book, on Coronavirus are thus suitable for the season, for people to learn, as well as, to release tension. The language of her poetry is simple and direct unlike most symbolic literary works. She employed both use of imagery and repetition especially, to achieve her rhythms and rhymes. In a culture where most people do not want to read, her language's readability is in fact common, ordinary and interesting.

The Anthology is also recommended for use in schools as it's about language, literature and history.

Professor S.N.A Agoro
Former Provost
Isaac Boro College of Education
Bayelsa State
Nigeria

INTRODUCTION

It had been over seven months, sometime in June 2019 since I had left Abuja for Port Harcourt, Nigeria following my last sabbatical holiday. I felt it's time to take a weekend short break and visit Abuja again; so my bag was packed for the weekend, with the mind to also attend some Christian events right there in Abuja.

However, God, the almighty and all knowing knew the break was going to be longer than imagined, as the Academic Staff Union of Universities (ASUU) to which I belong embarked on strike same week. While planning to stay back in Abuja until the University re-opens, suddenly the index case of the novel Coronavirus disease was announced in Lagos, Nigeria on Friday, February 28, 2020.

The Federal Ministry of Health had confirmed a coronavirus disease (COVID-19) case in Lagos State, Nigeria. The case, is the first case to be reported in Nigeria since the beginning of the outbreak in China in January 2020. It was a case of an Italian citizen who works in Nigeria and returned from Milan, Italy to Lagos, Nigeria on the 25th of February 2020. He was confirmed to have tested positive to covid19 by the Virology Laboratory of the Lagos University Teaching Hospital.

The Government of Nigeria thus assured all Nigerians of its preparedness since the first confirmation of cases in China, and how the government will use all its available resources to respond to this case. "We have already started working to identify all the contacts of the patient, since he entered Nigeria"; we were assured.

The Coronavirus pandemic sweeping the nations of the world has become overwhelming everywhere including our Nigeria. It was followed by national lockdown in Nigeria and in the quest for what next to do as a linguist and poet, the idea came, the thoughts kept coming, the ink kept flowing as I was listening to the television and reading on the social media, and I kept writing, tabbing on my tablet.

So, that was how I simply got stuck in Abuja; thanks to Pastor Bolu Olutayo and Pastor Dayo Olutayo who hosted me in Utako, Abuja as always; and prepared for me a conducive room and atmosphere in the quietness of their beautiful home where these narrative poems were written within four weeks from March 24th - April 26th 2020.

Enjoy it!

Funmilayo Adesanya-Davies
Port Harcourt
Nigeria
April 27th 2020

Coronavirus Says, The Voice Of The Martyrs Still Cry!

The voice of the martyrs still cry ...
All animals are now finally equal,
There is no threat to extinct only the Christians specie from the planet earth again,
Christians are no more the most endangered specie on the planet, but us all.

Coronavirus says, If we all die, we all die!

A Christian is positive
A Muslim is positive
A Pagan is positive
A Christian nation is positive
A Muslim nation is positive
A Pagan nation is positive!

Coronavirus says, If we all die, we all die!

A president is now in a common man's hospital
A senator is in common man's hospital
A politician is in common man's hospital
A civil servant is in common man's hospital
The poor is in common man's hospital
The rich is in common man's hospital!

Coronavirus says, If we all die, we all die!

Oh! No more sharing of money by Islamists
Ah! No more sharing of booties by Jihadists
So! No more sharing of ransom by Bandits
Oh! No more sharing of fidya by Marauders
Ah! No more sharing of aljawari by Nomads
Fulani herdsmen all back to their bushes
Boko Haram all ran back to their forests
ISWAP now all ran back to their hideouts!

Coronavirus says, If we all die, we all die!

In Nigeria:
I wish the virus could hold Fulani herdsmen hostage and demand ransoms

I wish the coronavirus could hold Miyetti Allah hostage and demand ransoms
I wish the virus could hold Boko Haram hostage and demand ransoms
I wish the coronavirus could hold ISWAP hostage and demand ransoms!

In the world :
I wish the virus could hold ISIS hostage and demand ransoms
I wish the virus could hold Al-Qaeda hostage and demand ransoms
I wish the coronavirus could hold Al-Shabaab hostage and demand ransoms!
Coronavirus says, If we all die, we all die!

It could have helped us get our blood shed back!
It could have helped us get our stolen wealth back!
It could have helped us get our lowered esteem back!

Coronavirus says, If we all die, we all die!

For the first time in mankind's history,
Islamists are getting silenced...
Until you give birth to a new world,
Stay on coronavirus...

Where man does not shout allahu akbar!
Where man does not shout allahu akbar!

 Where man does not shout allahu akbar!!!
While they behead others, and shout ALLAU AKBAR!
Stay on coronavirus!

Coronavirus says, If we all die, we all die!

The voice of the martyrs still cry ...
All animals are now finally equal,
There is no threat to extinct only the Christians specie from the planet earth,
Christians are no more the most endangered specie on the planet earth, BUT US ALL.

WE ALL ARE!!!

Coronavirus says, If we all die, we all die!

Author notes: (The Voice of the martyrs still cry!
Dedicated to all world Christian martyrs.
A THANK YOU NOTE TO DONALD TRUMP
March 25, 2020.)

If I were a Nigerian No1 Leader, With Coronavirus!

by Funmi Ade-Davies on March 25, 2020. © Mercy Funmilayo Adesanya-Davies, All rights reserved

I will let Nigeria be one again!

If I were a Nigerian No1 leader, with coronavirus,
I will end ceaseless abductions by Boko Haram!
If I were a Nigerian leader, with coronavirus,
I will end calculated kidnappings by ISWAP!
If I were a Nigerian leader, with coronavirus,
I will end casual beheadings by Islamic insurgents!

I will let Nigeria be one again!

If I were a Nigerian No1 leader, with coronavirus,
I will end abduction of girls as sex slaves!
If I were a Nigerian leader, with coronavirus,
I will end daily kidnapping and raping of women!
If I were a Nigerian leader, with coronavirus,
I will end capturing of boys as slaves and converts,
If I were a Nigerian leader, with coronavirus,
I will end capturing of men and beheading them!

I will let Nigeria be one again!

If I were a Nigerian No1 leader, with coronavirus,
I will end Boko Haram insurgents take over!
If I were a Nigerian leader, with coronavirus,
I will end ISWAP insurgents mass terrorism!
If I were a Nigerian leader, with coronavirus,
I will end Fulani herdsmen over run!

I will let Nigeria be one again!

If I were a Nigerian No1 leader, with coronavirus,
I will end Jihadists terrorism!
If I were a Nigerian leader, with coronavirus,
I will end Miyetti Allah harassment!
If I were a Nigerian leader, with coronavirus,

I will end Islamist religion agenda!

I will let Nigeria be one again!

If I were a Nigerian N1 leader, with coronavirus,
I will end Islamisation and Fulanisation of Nigeria!
If I were a Nigerian leader, with coronavirus,
I will end Africanisation, Arabialisation of Nigeria!
This is our time, this is like a proverb, this is a sign!
I will let Nigeria be in Peace,
I will let Nigeria be FREE again!

Author notes : (The Voice of martyrs still cry!
Dedicated to all Nigerian Christian martyrs.
BUT God, you are No1 leader of Nigeria!
March 25, 2020.)

There should be no more killings, With Coronavirus!

by Funmi Ade-Davies on March 27, 2020. © Mercy Funmilayo Adesanya-Davies, All rights reserved

The Voice of martyrs in Nigeria still cry!
There should be no more kidnappings of Christians,
with Coronavirus!
There should be no more killings of Christians,
with Coronavirus!
There should be no more beheadings of Christians,
with Coronavirus!
There should be no more religious cleansings of Christians, with Coronavirus!
There should be no more ethnic cleansings of Christians, with Coronavirus!

No more Boko Haram insurgents, with this Coronavirus!
No more ISWAP terrorists, with this Coronavirus!
No more Armed bandits, with this Coronavirus!
No more Herdsmen jihadists with this Coronavirus!
No more Miyetti Allah hostages, with this Coronavirus!
No more ISIS, with this Coronavirus!
No more El-Shabbab, with this Coronavirus!
No more Al-Qaeda, with this Coronavirus!

With Coronavirus, no more sharing of money!
With Coronavirus, no more sharing of booties!
With Coronavirus, no more sharing of ransom!
With Coronavirus, no more sharing of fidya!
With Coronavirus, no more sharing of aljawarib!
With Coronavirus! No more shouts of allahu akbar!
With Coronavirus! While they behead Christians!!!

People that are killed by Boko Haram and Herdsmen are more than Coronavirus
deaths in Nigeria!
Christians that are killed by Boko Haram and ISWAP are more than Coronavirus
deaths in Nigeria!!
Soldiers that are killed by Boko Haram and Bandits are more than Coronavirus deaths
in Nigeria!!!

If we acted swiftly, promptly and instantly against Boko Haram and Herdsmen as we
did to Coronavirus,

If we had acted quickly, speedily and drastically against Boko Haram and Bandits as
we did to Coronavirus,
If we acted immediately, hastily, and instantly against Boko Haram and Jihadists as
we did to Coronavirus,
Nigeria Christians could have been safe and delivered,
Nigeria could have finished with the issue of insecurity long ago!
So, why not grant forgiveness to repentant Coronaviruses,
Rehabilitate them,
Set them free,
And let then go back to the Nigerian society!
The Voice of martyrs in Nigeria still cry!

Author notes : (The Voice of martyrs still cry!
Dedicated to all Christian martyrs in Northern Nigeria.
A THANK YOU NOTE TO DONALD TRUMP
March 27, 2020.)

Coronavirus: They Knew It, China!

They knew it, China!
They pre-know it!
They premeditated it!

They willed it, China!
They forecasted it!
They planned it!

They deliberated it, China!
They considered it!
They anticipated!

The expected it, China!
They awaited it!
They projected it!

They organised it!
They arranged it!
They designed it!
They calculated it, China!

They set it out!
They lined it up!
They worked it out!
They thought it out, China!

They reasoned it!
They rationalised it!
They weighed it!
They studied it, China!
Could it be non-deliberate, no!
Could it be unintentional, no!
Could it be incidental, no!
Could it be accidental, no!

at random, no!

by chance, no!
abrupt, no!
sudden, no!
No, No, No!

It was their original fundamental inventive pivotal!
It was their prepared exploratory theorization!
It was their precursor preliminary most tested pilot!
It was their potential possible prospective arrangements!
It was their impending imminent projected invention!
After ensuing eventual ultimate intention!

So, so sad!
They planned it, sad!
So, so sad, China!

Author notes : (A dedication to All Who Knew It Not.
March 29, 2020.)

COVID-19: Coronavirus, China!

by Funmi Ade-Davies on March 29, 2020. © Mercy Funmilayo Adesanya-Davies, All rights reserved

Chinavirus!
Coronavirus, China!
Chinavirus!

China!
Oh, China!
They knew!
They knew it!
They knew it, China!
They knew it!
They knew!
Oh, China!
China!

The knew coronavirus!
The knew COVID-19!
They eat Rats,
They eat Bats,
They eat Snakes,
They eat Pangolins,
They eat Civets,
They eat Horses,
They eat Pigs!

The knew Coronavirus!
They knew Wuhanvirus!
The knew Chinavirus!
The knew COVID-19!
They eat fresh blood!
They eat all manner of raw animals !
They eat them all uncooked!

China!
Oh, China!

They knew!
They knew it!
They knew it, China!
They knew it!
They knew!
Oh, China!
China!

Chinavirus!
Coronavirus, China!
Chinavirus!
Wuhanvirus COVID-19.

Author notes : (A dedication to All Outside China/Wuhan, COVID-D Who Knew It Not. March 29, 2020.)

The Whole World Tolls As The Graveyard!

The whole world tolls as the graveyard,
With Donald Trump of USA doing his best,
Together with Sergio Mattarella of Italy trying his best,
Along side Xi Jinping of China minding his best!

Here we get the full list here:
List of death by March 28th, 2020,
With Coronavirus trying its best!

US: 116, 505 cases, 1, 925 deaths
Italy: 92, 572 cases, 10, 023 deaths
China: 81, 999 cases, 3, 299 deaths

Spain: 72, 248 cases, 5, 812 deaths
Germany: 56, 202 cases, 203 deaths
France: 38, 105 cases, 2, 317 deaths

Iran: 36, 408 cases, 2, 517 deaths
UK: 17, 312 cases, 1, 021 deaths
Switzerland: 14, 076 cases, 264 deaths

Netherlands: 9, 819 cases, 640 deaths
South Korea: 9, 478 cases, 144 deaths
Belgium: 9, 134 cases, 353 deaths

Austria: 8, 188 cases, 68 deaths
Turkey: 7, 402 cases, 108 deaths
Canada: 5, 448 cases, 61 deaths

Portugal: 5, 170 cases, 100 deaths
Norway: 3, 981 cases, 23 deaths
Australia: 3, 640 cases, 14 deaths

Israel: 3, 619 cases, 12 deaths
Brazil: 3, 477 cases, 111 deaths
....

The whole world tolls as the graveyard,
As Coronavirus knows it best!
As Chinesevirus knows it best!
As Wuhanvirus knows it best!

No!
No Coronavirus!
No to Chinesevirus please!
There should be No More Chinavirus please!

No! No!
No Hantavirus!
No Hantavirus please!
And there should be No Hantavirus please!

No! No! No!

Author notes : (Curtesy: The Johns Hopkins tracker is a really useful tool to stay up with day to day global developments. It has an interactive map to show you the cases, deaths and recoveries by country, which allows you to zoom in to specific cities to see their figures too.) (A dedication to All Researchers as Johns Hopkins Hospital. March 29, 2020.)

COVID-19 Vaccine: Africans, Do not Take it!

by Funmi Ade-Davies on March 29, 2020. © Mercy Funmilayo Adesanya-Davies, All rights reserved

Africans, Do not Take it!
Africans, Do not Take it!
Africans, Do not Take it!

There are in:
US: 116, 505 cases, 1, 925 deaths,
Italy: 92, 572 cases, 10, 023 deaths,
China: 81, 999 cases, 3, 299 deaths,

Africans, Do not Take it!

There are in:
Spain: 72, 248 cases, 5, 812 deaths,
Germany: 56, 202 cases, 203 deaths,
France: 38, 105 cases, 2, 317 deaths Africans, Do not Take it!

Africans, Do not Take it!

There are in:
Iran: 36, 408 cases, 2, 517 deaths,
UK: 17, 312 cases, 1, 021 deaths,
Switzerland: 14, 076 cases, 264 deaths!

Africans, Do not Take it!

There are in:
Netherlands: 9, 819 cases, 640 deaths,
South Korea: 9, 478 cases, 144 deaths,
Belgium: 9, 134 cases, 353 deaths!

Africans, Do not Take it!

There are in:
Austria: 8, 188 cases, 68 deaths
Turkey: 7, 402 cases, 108 deaths

Canada: 5, 448 cases, 61 deaths!

Africans, Do not Take it!

There are in:
Portugal: 5, 170 cases, 100 deaths,
Norway: 3, 981 cases, 23 deaths,
Australia: 3, 640 cases, 14 deaths!

Africans, Do not Take it!
Africans, Do not Take it!
Africans, Do not Take it!

COVID-19 Vaccine: Africans, Do not Take it!

*Author notes : (A dedication to All Africans and Bill Gate during COVID-19
March 29, 2020.)*

COVID-19: She Carries Her Cane!

She carries her cane, on a daily walk,
With no goal but to kill, to steal and destroy,
The COVID-19, the Coronavirus,
First found in Wuhan Region,
Among the People's Republic of China,
Her feet speaks silent sermons,
Ever heard by man!

So as at today, on her daily walk,
She has spread 597, 267 infections,
She has killed 27, 365 persons,
With about 23,569 in critical condition,
With total of 412, 980 in mild condition,
And 133, 363 infected recovered or discharged,
All around the world,
Her feet speaks silent sermons,
Ever heard by man!

As she carries her cane, on a daily walk,
The United States tops the list, of highest infected persons,
With 104, 205 cases and 1,701 deaths,
Followed by Italy with 86, 498 cases of infection,
And world's highest death rates of 9,134.
And China which originated the virus ,has recorded 81,394 infections, and 3, 295 deaths up till date,
While Spain recorded the second highest death rate of 5, 138 and 65, 719 infections, up to date.

She carries her cane, on a daily walk,
So as at today, on her daily walk,
As she carries her cane, on a daily walk,
From town to cities, countries and continents
Nigeria is credited with "81" infections and 2 deaths,
Corona has affected a total of 196 countries,
And 193 are members of the United Nations,
Her feet speaks silent sermons,
Ever heard by man!

As she carries her cane, on a daily walk,
And on, and on and on she goes...
With her virus, sickness, symptoms of death,
And deaths and the deaths continued to multiply,
Throughout the entire planet earth, increasing ...
Her feet speaks silent sermons,
Ever heard by man!

Author notes : (A Dedication To All Victims of Coronavirus with HEARTFELT SYMPATHY, Sunday March 29, 2020.)

Mr. Koro (Coronavirus) likes Billion too much o!

Koro, you too like money,
Mr. Koro, you too like money,
Mrs. Koro, you too like money!
Kororo Koro, ha, Owo!
Kokoro jowo jowo!

Haba! Money, you too,
You too like Koro,
Money, you too like Koro!
As Koro, Koro like money!
Kokoro jowo jowo!

Koro likes Billion too much o!
Mr. Koro likes Billion too much o!
Mrs. Koro likes Billion too much o!
For Nigeria nikan,
Ni Nigeria nikan,
In Nigeria alone:
See the contribution wey you day take:
Number them one by one:
1. Aliko Dangote   -1Billion.
2. Abdulsamad Rabiu - 1Billion.
3. Femi Otedola   -1Billion.
4. Tony OElumelu   -1Billion.
5. Herbert O. Wigwe - 1Billion.
6. Segun Agbaje   - 1Billion.
7. Jim Ovia   - 1Billion.
8. Access Bank   - 1Billion.
9. GT Bank   -1Billion.
10. Zenith Banks   -1Billion.
11. Atiku Abubakar -50million.
12. UBA.   - 2.5 Billion
13. NNPC.   - 11 Billion
14.Bar Robinson Ozomma Akpua 10M
15.Chief Obiorah Okonkwo-200M
16.Idris Garuba -170M

17.Babatunde oshinowo-500M
18.Engr Autor Eze-500M
19.Igwe Mac Anthony Okonkwo Igwe Alor-40M
20.Mrs Bola Adabisi -70M
21. Hon Osita Ejideaku- 25M
22. Dr John Olaru -55M
23: ChuksKamzy Inverter Solar Technologies. 900 Billion
24.Mrs TJ Tom-Bright-35M
25.Chief OG Ezeaku-30M
26. Mr. Chidi Ozor. - 4Billion
27. Mr. Chinedu obi 70Billion naira
28. Mr. Onyegbule Durugbo(Bryanz Nig Ltd 3Billion
29. Chief Ofodum Ifeanyi. One Billion
30. Engr. Oluwadante Dickson 20 million
31. Mrs Ebony Njoku -60M.
A ti bee bee lo....

Beeni,
Koro no dey ask for money,
Koro no dey beg for money,
Koro no dey accept money,
Koro no dey look for money!

Beeni,
Koro no dey ask for money,
Mr. Koro no dey beg for money,
Mrs. Koro no dey accept money,
Na, Money dey look for Koro!
Na, Money dey look for Mr. Koro o!
Na, Money dey look Mrs. for Koro!

Why I no be like Koro!
Why you no be like Koro!
Why we no be as Koro o!
Kokoro jowo jowo o!

From individuals, Koro
From government, Koro
From corporate, Koro
From politician, Koro
From business, Koro
From businesses men, Koro
From nationals, Koro

From internationals Koro!

For village, Koro
For town, Koro
For City, Koro
For County, Koro
For Country , Koro
For Continent, Koro!

From White, Koro
From Black, Koro
From Rich, Koro
From poor, Koro
From Millionaire, Koro
From Billionaire, Koro!

Koro, you too like money o,
Mr. Koro, you too like money o,
Mrs. Koro, you too like money o!
Kororo Koro, ha, Owo o!
Kokoro jowo jowo!

Mr. Koro likes billion too much o!

Author notes : Dedicated to all the millionaires and billionaires and others in Nigeria who care to donate for COVID-19 survival. Thank you! APRIL 1, 2020.

Coronavirus Lockdown, Everything aren't Lockdown!

by Funmi Ade-Davies on April 1, 2020. © Mercy Funmilayo Adesanya-Davies, All rights reserved

Lockdown!
Lockdown!
Lockdown!

The whole world in a lockdown!
As everything seems lockdown!
But somethings are not lockdown!

But remember,

Sunrise is not locked down,
Gentle rain is not locked down,
Quiet breeze is not locked down,
Sunset is not locked down!

Morning is not locked down,
Afternoon is not locked down,
Daytime is not locked down,
Evening is not locked down!

Smile is not locked down,
Laughter is not locked down,
Love is not locked down,
Family time is not locked down,
Relationship is not locked down!

Creativity is not locked down,
Learning is not locked down,
Conversation is not locked down,
Imagination is not locked down,
Thinking is not locked down,
Reading is not locked down,
Writing is not locked down!

Praying is not locked down,
Meditation is not locked down,

Singing is not locked down,
Sleeping is not locked down,
Resting is not locked down,
Quietness is not locked down,
Calmness is not locked down!

Righteous is not locked down,
Kindness is not locked down,
Peace is not locked down,
Joy is not locked down,
Mercy is not locked down,
Hope is not locked down,
Comfort is not locked down,
Faith is not locked down!

The whole world in a lockdown!
As everything seems lockdown!
But most things are not lockdown!

Lockdown!
Lockdown!
Lockdown!

Author notes : (A dedication to All Who Choose to stay home during the lockdown!)

COVID-19: We Must Find A Solution!

Chinesevirus
Coronavirus
Chinavirus
COVID-D
The C.V!

As MERS, and as SARS!
As the Common flu, ever well known!
A mutant Coronavirus flew in!
Attacking the respiratory system right in!

Someone tweaked it to increase!
Someone tweaked the virus to increase!
Someone tweaked that virus to increase!

With 2-14 days incubation period to produce!
To attack the lungs directly within just 5 minutes!
To terminate life instantly for no cause!

A manipulated virus!
A man made virus!
A made virus!

To what end!
For their economic gains!
Just for no just cause!

We have found the town, Wuhan,
We have found the country, China,
We have found the people, Chinese,

We must find a solution!
We must find an end!
We must find a solution to it!
We must find an end to this!

The world must fight it to a stand still!
The world must fight it to a conclusive end!
The world must fight it to an end!

Chinesevirus
Coronavirus
Chinavirus
COVID-D
The C.V!

Author notes : (Dedicated to a 2019 leaked movie/film from China.
A THANK YOU NOTE TO DONALD TRUMP
March 30, 2020.)

The Cruel Covid-19!

The cruel and dangerous COVID-19
The harmful and lethal COVID-19
The hurried but invisible killer COVID-19
We shall say goodbye to you very soon!

Many are dead at your stance
They died with your sting without restraint
Dead with your death on planned they all go
Dying untimely with your hurting deathblows
Your unkind deathblows to all mankind.

We shall say goodbye to you very soon!

Companies around the world are racing
They are racing to develop cures and vaccines
They launched early safety testing and safety tips
But experts say they need to develop a vaccine
Which will sure take a while to test.

We shall say goodbye to you very soon!

Russia's Federal Biomedical Agency,
Developed a drug for the treatment,
The drug they said was based on mefloquine,
A brother prevention to treating malaria
To provide an effective treatment for you
For COVID-19 patients with varying severity
Your treatment, oh COVID-19!

We shall say goodbye to you very soon!

Such drug as it prevents virus replication in cells
Such drug will stop the inflammatory process caused by the virus.
The drug Mefloquine has to be combined with antibiotics for the maximum effect,
Allowing an increase in the concentration of antiviral agents in blood plasma and lungs.

This will ensure effective treatment of patients with various degrees of coronavirus infection,
The treatment was developed taking Chinese and French experience into account,
Thanks to Veronika Skvortsova, the head of agency.

We shall say goodbye to you very soon!

Many are dead, several are gone
They died with your sting
With your death on planned
Dying with your severe deathblows
Your unkind deathblows to all mankind.

The cruel and destructive COVID-19
The harmful and fatal COVID-19
The hurried but invisible killer COVID-19
We'll all soon say goodbye to you!

Author notes : Dedicated with thanks to Veronika Skvortsova, A WOMAN, the head of Agency - Russia's Federal Biomedical Agency, March, 30 2020

COVID-19: As I Watch You Spread!

by Funmi Ade-Davies on April 2, 2020. © Mercy Funmilayo Adesanya-Davies, All rights reserved

Chinesevirus as I watch you spread,
deeply I mourn,
Chinavirus as we watch you spread,
deeply we mourn,
Coronavirus they watch you spread,
deeply they mourn.

Chinese is suddenly attached,
Americans is seriously lamenting,
Italians are massively dying,
Spaniards are crying,
Nigerians are struggling.

Everywhere:
Shops are closing,
Companies are loosing,
Streets are emptying,
Sanitizer are Selling,
Gloves are reigning.
Masks are moving!

Online:
News are spreading,
Callers and texting,
Bloggers are blogging,
Youths are tweeting,
Facebookers are posting,
Whatsappers are broadcasting.

In Nigeria:
Mohammadu Buhari Is lagging,
Aba Kyari is dying,
Seyi Makinde is recovering,
Bala Muhammad is resting,
Babajide Sanwoolu is trying,
NCDC Is Announcing...

In Africa:
W.H.O is watching,
Suspects are testing,
Victims are isolating,
Everyone is hiding,
Everybody is running.

In the whole world:
Everyone is watching, praying and repenting.

Chinesevirus as I watch you spread,
deeply I mourn,
Chinavirus as we watch you spread,
deeply we mourn,
Coronavirus they watch you spread,
deeply they mourn.

Abide with me Lord, COVID-19 No Coronavirus

Abide with me, fast falls Coronavirus Covid-19
The darkness of Covid-19 deepens

Lord, with me please abide
When other helpers fail and comforts flee
Help of the helpless, oh, abide with me against Covid-19

Swift to its ebbs, fast falls Coronavirus Covid-19
Earth's joys grow deepens dim, with Covid-19
Lord, with me please abide
Change and decay in all around I see
O Thou who changest not, abide with me
against Covid-19

I fear no foe, with Thee at hand of Coronavirus Covid-19
Ills have no weight, and tears no bitterness
Lord, with me please abide
Where is death's sting? where, grave, thy victory?
I triumph still, if Thou abide with me
against Covid-19

Hold Thou Thy cross before the Coronavirus Covid-19
Shine through the gloom and point me to the skies
Lord, with me please abide
In life, in death, o Lord, abide with me
Abide with me, abide with me
against Covid-19.

Author notes: (Dedicated to the Songwriters: Henry Francis Lyte / Will Henry Monk. Abide with Me lyrics © Universal Music Publishing Group, Sony/ATV Music Publishing LLC, Kobalt Music Publishing Ltd.)

Coronavirus: The Fear Alone!

The fear of the pickup
the fear of the test
the fear of the diagnoses
the fear of isolation
the fear of 14 days stay
the fear of kitting up
the fear of self care!

The fear of these fears alone
Are nothing but fear
It's nothing but fearful!

The fear of the result
the fear of the sickness
the fear of the pains
the fear of the agony
the fear of stigmatization
the fear of marginalization
the fear of sudden death!

The fear of these fears alone
Are nothing but fear
It's nothing but fearful!

The fear of feeling sick
the fear of itching throat
the fear of dry throat
the fear of dry cough
the fear of high temperature
the fear of shortness of breath
the fear of loss of smell and taste!

The fear of these fears alone
Are nothing but fear!
It's nothing but fearful!

The fear of constant cough
the fear of running nose

the fear of continuous vomit
the fear of the diarrhea
the fear of respiratory syndrome
the fear of gasping
and fatigue
the fear of breathing on oxygen!

The fear of these fears alone
Are nothing but real fear
It's nothing but fearful!

The fear of serious fever
the fear of pneumonia
the fear of breathing difficulty
the fear of the lungs infection
the fear of other infections
the fear of other complications
the fear of uttermost death!

The fear of these fears alone
Are nothing but real fear
It's nothing but fearful!

The fear of the hospital environment
the fear of stressful nurses
the fear of other patients
the fear of the isolation centre
the fear of care givers costumes
the fear of doctors demeanour
the fear of mass burial!

The fear of these fears also
Are nothing but real fear!
It's nothing but fearful!

The fear of the no visitors
the fear of stressful no visitations
the fear of no family members
the fear of no friends
the fear of no acquaintances
the fear of no neighbours
the fear of no great neighbourhood!

The fear of these fears also
Are nothing but real fear!
It's nothing but fearful!

The fear of no prevention
the fear of no medication
the fear of prescription
the fear of no medicine
the fear of no vaccine
the fear of no cure
the fear of possible death!

The fear of these fears alone
Are nothing but fear
It's nothing but fearful!

The fear of hand washing
the fear of mask wearing
the fear of gloves swearing
the fear of no to touching
the fear of no to coughing
the fear of no to face touching
the fear of separation!

The fear of these fears also
Are nothing but real fear!
It's nothing but fearful!

The fear of not surviving
the fear of not making it
the fear of passing on
the fear of death
the fear of eternity
the fear of hades
the fear of hell!
The fear of these fears also
Are nothing but fear
It's nothing but fearful!

Fear
the fear
oh fear
fearful in themselves
dreadful all the way
oh! Lord have mercy
so help us Lord
Deliver us God!

Author notes: (Dedicated to the Coronavirus COVID-19 Survivors)
(Advice: Let's all get born again thus vaccinated with the precious blood of Jesus Christ!!! Hebrews 2:15 KJV:
"And deliver them who through fear of death were all their lifetime subject to bondage." HAPPY PALM
SUNDAY April 5, 2020.)

Oh Wuhan Conspiracy!

by Funmi Ade-Davies on April 5, 2020. © Mercy Funmilayo Adesanya-Davies, All rights reserved

Oh Wuhan Conspiracy!

Conspiracy of don't touch yourself
Conspiracy of don't touch your face
Conspiracy of don't touch your mouth
Conspiracy of don't touch nostrils
Conspiracy of don't touch eyes
Why not!

Oh Wuhan Conspiracy!

Conspiracy of don't touch yourselves
Conspiracy of don't touch one another
Conspiracy of don't handshake each other
Conspiracy of no kissing and pecking
Conspiracy of no touching and hogging
Why not!
Oh Wuhan Conspiracy!

Conspiracy of don't touch me I don't touch you
Conspiracy of virus and sickness
Conspiracy of illness and weakness
Conspiracy of grave and deaths
Conspiracy of death and mass burials
Why these!

Thou Wuhan Conspiracy!

Wash your hands and wear your gloves
How many times daily?
Wear your face masks and use your sanitizer
How many times weekly?
Do your coronavirus test and know your status
How many times monthly?
Don't travel but stay in your house!
How many times yearly

I ask you!

Thou Wuhan Conspiracy!

For how long is this for
For how long will this be
For how long could this last
For how long would this end
For how long should this endure!
I ask you!

Thou Wuhan Conspiracy!

Author notes : Dedicated to those who believe in
"The Wuhan Conspiracy!" (USA just discovered the man who manufactured and sold the Corona virus to
China. Dr. Charles Lieber, Head of the chemistry and biology department at Harvard University, USA. He was
just arrested according to American department sources).

Coronavirus: My Experience on the Street of Lagos

It was time to sleep, as usual
Just after I took my shower
Just before I lie on my bed
I took my phone to off by a click
Then comes in a flash right on the phone,
another message to read, I must
A storyline I just must not ignore
And maybe you need to read it too:

"It is no longer a news that Lagos state is partially shut down and that the Lagos state government has ordered that all shops and markets should be closed due to the current outbreak of Covid19 (Corona virus).

Yesterday, I was on the street of Lagos and I couldn't get a bus at some point of which I had to trek.

It got to a point where I was so thirsty and I couldn't get a shop to buy water, as all the shops I came across were locked and I couldn't bear the thirst.

As I was trekking and sweating profusely, then a thought came to me "Goodness! hope rapture has not happened sha?"

Immediately I stopped and I noticed that only few people were on the streets.

The Lagos I use to know to be so busy, that you had to struggle to find your way in places like Oshodi, Eko Idumota e.t.c. is now having few people on the street.

At first I was like "Abi Rapture don happen ni? Am I dreaming or is this a reality?"

As I was asking myself series of questions, I saw some policemen attached to the Lagos state task force, destroying properties of some stubborn traders who were sneaking to sell goods and they were forcing them to obey the Government's directives.

When I saw what the policemen were doing, my mind went to the role that Anti Christ will be playing after the rapture.

As I continued in my journey, I needed to enter a bank to perform some transactions.

I was about entering the bank when I noticed a security guard held me back, asking if

I had sanitized my hands.

When I told him I haven't, he 'bounced' me out of the door and I was directed to the point where hand sanitizer was placed.

As I applied the sanitizer on my palm, then I remembered what the scripture said about the mark of the beast (666).

It got dawn on me that as I was not allowed to enter the Bank because I haven't sanitized my hand.

It's the same way people won't be able to transact except they receive the mark "666".

After I sanitized my hand, the security guard smiled at me and became more friendly with me.

I was welcomed back to the door and I entered into the bank.

Beloved, all we are experiencing now is a glimpse of what will happen after rapture.

It will be a disaster if anyone misses the rapture.

Covid19 will soon go but what if Rapture takes place now, will you be rapturable?

Remember that the rapture will not take place twice, it is once. And
It is only those who have identified with Christ that will be rapturable.

Have you given your life to Christ?
Its not about going to Church or been a worker in Church, heaven knows those who have truly accepted Christ.

Today is the day of Salvation, don't procrastinate.

All over the world people are afraid of contracting Covid-19 and they are buying face masks, sanitizers and also been careful but the question is, ARE WE NOT Also Afraid OF Missing Heaven OR Rapture When IT Takes Place?

IF YOU Miss Heaven, YOU Will NOT Miss Hell
Think about this."

Author notes : (Dedicated to the Story teller ...from Lagos Nigeria on Coronavirus Pandemic.)

COVID-19: Why GOD'S Anger Has Befallen The World!

by Funmi Ade-Davies on April 5, 2020. © Mercy Funmilayo Adesanya-Davies, All rights reserved

COVID-19: Why GOD'S Anger Has Befallen The World!

Burning Bibles is openly witnessed in Uganda and beheading of Christians every where in their numbers, Christians and the most endangered specie on the planet earth. God is never happy his are despised, for He is the creator and owner of the heaven and the earth!

COVID-19: Why GOD'S Anger Has Befallen The World!

Adultery is tolerated now in the world and publicly allowed in South Africa, incest is normal, homosexuality is not a shame.

COVID-19: Why GOD'S Anger Has Befallen The World!

The United States confirmed that for all countries in the
world to build good relations with the great power, these countries must practice
homosexual marriage (woman + woman = 1 or Man + man = 1).

COVID-19: Why GOD'S Anger Has Befallen The World!

Germany had just signed the law which declares
that there is no more incest, that is to say: Brother and
Sister can get married, Mum with her son and
Dad with his daughter.

COVID-19: Why GOD'S Anger Has Befallen The World!

The City of Miami is now proclaimed a City of public sex which means that on the road, church, market, football field etc. if you need sex you can have it en route without having any problem.

COVID-19: Why GOD'S Anger Has Befallen The World!

Canada allows bestiality (sex with Animals) In Spain: pornographic films are allowed in high school and universities.

COVID-19: Why GOD'S Anger Has Befallen The World!

The authorization of the prostitution of minors,
Marg Luker declares that any young girl at the age of 10 feels sexual pleasure and no
one should deny that person from discovering how her body works.

COVID-19: Why GOD'S Anger Has Befallen The World!

Finally, the US has opened the church of satan publicly. Dear brothers and sisters, the
end is near, the departure in the Glory approaches.

COVID-19: Why GOD'S Anger Has Befallen The World!

Author notes :(A dedication to you writer, who said inspired me by said, "Send this message to your friends or will you ignore it? Jesus said, "If you deny me before your friends, I will deny you before my father.") (Read more: Nahum1:3 and 2 Chronicles 7:14).

Is Coronavirus linked To 5G Masts? Debunk the myths!

Is it in Conspiracy theories that coronavirus are linked to 5G masts?
Or its in fact that 5G masts are linked to coronavirus?

Debunk the myths!
Debunk the truths!
Debunk the facts!

Conspiracy theorists claimed 5G are being emitted was not sparking coronavirus.
Non-Conspiracy theorists claimed 5G being emitted was sparking coronavirus.

Debunk the myths!
Debunk the truths!
Debunk the facts!

Says there is no scientific evidence that 5G technology poses any threat to human health and it was confirmed as safe by the radiation watchdog last month.

Debunk the myths!
Debunk the truths!
Debunk the facts!

MobileUK, the trade organisation representing Three, O2, EE and Vodafone, says such is untruths and said some of the industry's key workers are being abused over the unfounded 5G myths.

Debunk the myths!
Debunk the truths!
Debunk the facts!

Says 'Research into the safety of radio signals including 5G, which has been conducted for more than 50 years, has led to the establishment of human exposure standards including safety factors that protect against all established health risks."

Debunk the myths!
Debunk the truths!
Debunk the facts!

Says, "Mobile UK said: 'It is concerning that certain groups are using the Covid-19 pandemic to spread false rumours and theories about the safety of 5G technologies."

Debunk the myths!
Debunk the truths!
Debunk the facts!

5G staff says, 'More worryingly some people are also abusing our key workers and making threats to damage infrastructure under the pretence of claims about 5G.

Debunk the myths!
Debunk the truths!
Debunk the facts!

Says, 'This is not acceptable and only impacts on our ability as an industry to maintain the resilience and operational capacity of the networks to support mass home working and critical connectivity to the emergency services, vulnerable consumers and hospitals."

Debunk the myths!
Debunk the truths!
Debunk the facts!

Says, "The theories that are being spread about 5G on social media are baseless and are not grounded in accepted scientific theory."

Debunk the myths!
Debunk the truths!
Debunk the facts!

Author notes : (Dedicated to 5G only if it's not connected to CORONAVIRUS outbreak. Thanks)

Coronavirus: My Ways Are Not Your Ways!

by Funmi Ade-Davies on April 5, 2020. © Mercy Funmilayo Adesanya-Davies, All rights reserved

CORONAVIRUS: My Ways Are Not Your Ways!*

For my thoughts are not your thoughts,
Neither are your ways my ways,
Saith the Lord.

For as the heavens are higher than the earth,
So are my ways higher than your ways,
And my thoughts than your thoughts,
Saith the Lord.

For as the rain cometh down, and the snow from heaven,
And returneth not thither, but watereth the earth,
And maketh it bring forth and bud,
That it may give seed to the sower,
And bread to the eater.
Saith the Lord.

CORONAVIRUS may end today
CORONAVIRUS may end tomorrow
CORONAVIRUS may end after one week

CORONAVIRUS may end after one month
CORONAVIRUS may end after one year
CORONAVIRUS might end after one decade
CORONAVIRUS might end after one century
CORONAVIRUS might never end forever
CORONAVIRUS never ever end for ever
CORONAVIRUS might never end for ever and ever CORONAVIRUS never end for ever and ever and ever!

So shall my word be that goeth forth out of my mouth,
It shall not return unto me void,
But it shall accomplish that which I please,

And it shall prosper in the thing whereto I sent it.
For an everlasting sign that shall not be cut off.

For my thoughts are not your thoughts,
Neither are your ways my ways,
saith   the Lord.

Author notes (With allusion to Isaiah 55:6-13 King James Version (KJV).@ Funmilayo Adesanya-Davies (A Dedication To All Victims who are destined to have CORONAVIRUS with HEARTFELT SYMPATHY, April 3, 2020.)

Coronavirus Says You Should Stay Home, To Care!

by Funmi Ade-Davies on April 5, 2020. © Mercy Funmilayo Adesanya-Davies, All rights reserved

51

Coronavirus says you should stay home, To Care

Coronavirus says you should stay home
Stay home, but do not choke him
Stay home, and enjoy the lockdown.

Coronavirus says you should stay home
Stay home, but do not fight her
Stay home, and enjoy the lockdown.

To all couples, families, and friends
It's more time to love and to care:
Its time to stay at home, to bound and
be knitted together.

To all couples, families, and friends
It's more time to love and to care:
It's no time for domestic violence to shatter
the lives of loved ones.

Coronaviruses says you should stay home
Stay home, and show him love
Stay home, and enjoy the lockdown.

Coronaviruses says you should stay home
Stay home, and show her love
Stay home, and enjoy the lockdown.

Coronaviruses says you should stay at home, to care.

Author notes : (A dedication to all world families as they enjoy the lockdown by Coronavirus pandemic.)

Coronavirus: Covid-19 Conspiracy Theories

The list are endless, 123... go!
The brainstorming has no end...

The virus is caused by 5G, they are using the opportunity of people staying indoors to lay 5G cables.

China created the virus to dominate the West, and finally keep them under.

American soldiers that participated in the 2019 Wuhan Military World Games brought the virus to China.

The list are endless123... go!
The brainstorming has no end...

Bill Gates, and his likes and co created the virus as a population control scheme.

The New World Order will create a vaccine for the virus to rule the world.

The Democrats created the virus in conjunction with others to bring down the government of Donald Trump.

The list are endless 123... go!
The brainstorming has no end...

Donald Trump created the virus and waited till it spread so much in the USA, so he'll emerge victorious and win the November elections easily.

Coronavirus doesn't really exist; you only get it from the test kits.

There is no coronavirus at all in Nigeria, the government is simply using it to make their usual money.

Coronavirus doesn't exist, at all at all, it's all a scam!

The list are endless 123... go!
The brainstorming has no end...

Author notes : (A dedication to all brainstorming on the source, cause and origin of Coronavirus - As well as those compiling it! Thank you!)

All Terrorists Get Coronavirus, COVID -19!

by Funmi Ade-Davies on April 6, 2020. © Mercy Funmilayo Adesanya-Davies, All rights reserved

Boko Harams jihadists cannot not sneeze and cough into tissues or the crook of their elbow.

Boko Harams jihadists pour all mucus and spit on their skin all the away.

Boko Harams jihadists cannot avoid touching their face with unwashed hands all the time.

ISWAP terrorists cannot avoid close contact with people who are sick, because they must fight.

ISWAP terrorists cannot avoid close contact with people exhibiting respiratory symptoms and fever, because they must war.

ISWAP terrorists cannot avoid regularly and thoroughly clean surfaces with a disinfectant because they are illiterates.

Fulani herdsmen bandits cannot afford correct face masks, to prevent the spread of the virus, because they are dumb,

Fulani herdsmen bandits cannot avoid close contact with
people cold and flu, because they are adamant.

Fulani herdsmen bandits cannot avoid travelling from one place to another, which is the best way to stop the spread of coronavirus.

Boko Harams islamist, ISWAP terrorists and Fulani herdsmen bandits are thus a done deal to the Coronavirus,
COVID-19.

El-Shabbab, Al-Qaeda and ISIS terrorists are all thus a done deal for the Coronavirus,
COVID-19.

All Terrorists Get Coronavirus, COVID -19!

Author notes : (A Dedication to the Boko Haram, ISWAP and Fulani herdsmen bandits, ISIS, El-Shabbab, Al-Qaeda etc. terrorist groups as they unfailingly collide with the Coronavirus COVID-19 pandemic.)

Coronavirus Says You Should Stay Home, To Work!

by Funmi Ade-Davies on April 6, 2020. © Mercy Funmilayo Adesanya-Davies, All rights reserved

Coronavirus says you should stay home
Stay home, but do not be lazy and idle
Stay home, and enjoy the lockdown
Stay home, and be safe.

Coronavirus says you should stay home
Stay home, but do not be vain and empty
Stay home, and enjoy the lockdown
Stay home, and be safe.

To all families, friends and acquaintances:
It's time to push, work and toil
It's time to stay at home,
To be creative, ingenious and innovative.

To all families, friends and acquaintances:
It's time to push, work hard and toil
Its time to stay at home,
To be innovative, imaginative and inventive.

Coronaviruses says you should stay home
Stay home, but do not be blue and gloomy
Stay home, and enjoy the lockdown
Stay home, and be safe.

Coronaviruses says you should stay home
Stay home, but do not be indolent and depressed
Stay home, and enjoy the lockdown
Stay home, and be safe.

Coronaviruses says you should stay at home, to work.

Author notes : (A dedication to all world families as they enjoy the lockdown by Coronavirus pandemic to work.)

Donate to persecuted Christians!

by Funmi Ade-Davies on April 6, 2020. © Mercy Funmilayo Adesanya-Davies, All rights reserved

55

Donate to persecuted Christians
They don't need your sympathy

They need your money,
They need your support
They also need your help
They really need you help!

As coronavirus dying victims
They even dying more...
As coronavirus suffering victims
They also suffering a lot
Before the arrival of coronavirus
They had suffered the worst
And now, with coronavirus
They are suffering the more...

Donate to persecuted Christians
The don't need your sympathy

They need your money,
They need your support
They also need your help
They really need your help!

Author notes : (A dedication to All suffering and ALL RICH CHRISTIANS every where in the world, Curtesy COVID -19.)

Coronavirus: What led to what?

56

I am asking?

Did Conspiracy Theories lead to Coronavirus
Or Coronavirus led to the Conspiracy Theories!

Did Coronavirus lead to the Conspiracy Theories Or Conspiracy Theories led to Coronavirus!

Coronavirus: Which led to which?

I ask you!
You ask me!
They ask us!
We ask them!

Let's Create Coronavirus Rooms!

by Funmi Ade-Davies on April 8, 2020. © Mercy Funmilayo Adesanya-Davies, All rights reserved

It was all in my dream
We tried to a build house
Designed as a cure for Coronavirus COVID-19
And build and build to strength!

Let's create coronavirus free mobile rooms
Where one can pass and be clean!
Where one can walk through and be cleanse
Here and there and save ourselves
Let's create coronavirus free mobile rooms
All the stress!

Let's manufacture coronavirus rooms
Where one can pass and be clean!
Here and there and save ourselves
All the stress!

Let's invent coronavirus rooms
Where one can pass and be clean
Here and there and save ourselves
All the stress!

Where their is pencil,
There should be an eraser,
Where there is paint,
There should be a cleanser
Where there is sin
There should be blood of Jesus!

That's a room,

And that's our continuous PRAYER ROOM....

It's simple and short!

Coronavirus: Life is a Gift!

by Funmi Ade-Davies on April 10, 2020. © Mercy Funmilayo Adesanya-Davies, All rights reserved

From CORONAVIRUS PANDEMIC
Learn that:

Life is Gift
Life is a Gift
A gift of God
A special Gift from God
Life Is All that matters
Life is All
Respect others Lives!
So, Respect others Lives!

Life is a mystery
That is only know to God
Also known to Jesus who shed His blood
Known to Jesus
The only begotten Son of God!

Life is full of wonders
That no man can tell of
Life is filled with wonders
That no one could explain
That only God could tell of and explain
Life is such a mystery to me
Life should be a great mystery to you
Life should be mysterious to us all!

When I think about God's creation
Then I wonder how he made me and you
When I think about all the blessings on us
That God is pouring down unto the world
Over me an you!

Life is Gift
Life is a Gift
A gift of God

A special Gift from God
Life Is All that matters
Life is All
Respect others Lives!
So, Respect others Lives!

A LESSON CORONAVIRUS PANDEMIC!
WHAT A LESSON!

Author notes : (A dedication to ALL alive on 2020 Good Friday, April 10, 2020.)

COVID-19: Oh Happy Day at Easter!

by Funmi Ade-Davies on April 12, 2020. © Mercy Funmilayo Adesanya-Davies, All rights reserved

Despite COVID-19
Despite the Coronavirus
Despite SARS-CoV-2 Virus
Oh happy
Oh happy day!

Oh happy day at Easter
Oh happy Easter day
Oh happy resurrection day
When Jesus washed
When Jesus washed!

Oh happy day at Easter
Oh happy Easter day
Oh happy resurrection day
Jesus Christ washed my sins away, oh happy day
Jesus Christ washed my sins away, oh happy day!

Oh happy day at Easter
Oh happy Easter day
Oh happy resurrection day
He taught me how to watch, fast, fight and pray
He taught me how to watch, fast, fight and pray!

Oh happy day at Easter
Oh happy Easter day
Oh happy resurrection day
And live rejoicing everyday
And live rejoicing everyday!

Despite COVID-19
Despite the Coronavirus
Despite SARS-CoV-2 Virus
Oh happy
Oh happy day!

Remember resurrection into glory is always assured!

Author notes : (A dedication to ALL Christians at Easter April 10, 2020 during the Coronavirus pandemic outbreak..)

COVID-19: Christ Has Won The Victory!

61

COVID-19
Coronavirus, SAR-CoV-2
Christ Has Won The Victory!
Christ is risen! He is risen!
Tell it out with joyful voice.
He has burst his three days' prison;
Let the whole wide earth rejoice.
Death is conquered; man is free.
Christ has won the victory.
Christ Has Won The Victory!

COVID-19
Coronavirus, SAR-CoV-2
Christ Has Won The Victory!
Come with high and holy hymning;
Chant our Lord's triumphant lay.
Not one darksome cloud is dimming,
Yonder glorious morning ray,
Breaking o'er the purple east,
Symbol of our Easter feast.
Christ Has Won The Victory!

COVID-19
Coronavirus, SAR-CoV-2
Christ Has Won The Victory!
He is risen! He is risen!
He hath opened heaven's gate.
We are free from sin's dark prison,
Risen to a holier state.
And a brighter Easter beam,
On our longing eyes shall stream.
Christ Has Won The Victory!

Author notes (Dedicated to: Writers Cecil Frances Alexander, 1818–1895, Music: Joachim Neander, 1650–1680. EASTER Hymn on Easter day April 11, 2020.)

COVID-19: SARS-CoV-2 Virus outbreak!

by Funmi Ade-Davies on April 12, 2020. © *Mercy Funmilayo Adesanya-Davies, All rights reserved*

Praise the Lord! Praise the Lord! Let the earth hear His voice!
Praise the Lord! Praise the Lord! Let the people rejoice!
Come to the Father, through Jesus the Son:
Give Him the glory! Great things He has done!

Before the world plagues
Ahead of the coronavirus pandemic
SARS-CoV-2 Virus outbreak!

To God be the glory! Great things He has done!
So loved He the world that He gave us His Son;
Who yielded His life an atonement for sin,
And opened the life-gate that all may go in.

Before the world plagues
Ahead of the coronavirus pandemic
SARS-CoV-2 Virus outbreak!

O perfect redemption, the purchase of blood!
To every believer the promise of God;
The vilest offender who truly believes,
That moment from Jesus a pardon receives.

Before the world plagues
Ahead of the coronavirus pandemic
SARS-CoV-2 Virus outbreak!

Before the world plagues
Ahead of the coronavirus pandemic
SARS-CoV-2 Virus outbreak!

Great things He has taught us, great things He has done,
And great our rejoicing through Jesus the Son;
But purer, and higher, and greater will be;
Our wonder, our worship, when Jesus we see.

Before the world plagues
Ahead of the coronavirus pandemic
SARS-CoV-2 Virus outbreak!

Praise the Lord! Praise the Lord! Let the earth hear His voice!
Praise the Lord! Praise the Lord! Let the people rejoice!
Come to the Father, through Jesus the Son:
Give Him the glory! Great things He has done!

Author notes : (Dedication to Source: Musixmatch, Songwriters: James F. Hammerly / Fanny Crosby / William Doane, To God Be the Glory lyrics © Dayspring Music Llc, Word Music, Llc, Fred Bock Music Co.,inc., Dayspring Music, Llc.)

COVID-19 Confession: I Shall Not Die!

by Funmi Ade-Davies on April 12, 2020. © Mercy Funmilayo Adesanya-Davies, All rights reserved

I shall not die
I shall not die but live
I shall not die but live to declare the glory of the Lord
You shall not die
They shall not die but live
We shall not die but live to declare the glory of the Lord
In the land of the living, amen.
From SARS-CoV-2 Virus outbreak
From Coronavirus, COVID-19.
I shall not die in Jesus mighty and precious name, amen.
Happy Resurrection!

I believe and so I declare:

The Lord is my Rock. He is large and solid for me. He can hold me just as I can hold Him. I choose to hold on to Him and His word in the name of Jesus Christ my Lord.

The Lord is my Fortress. He is my stronghold and defence headquarters. As long as I am in Him, no plague can penetrate me. I am safe in Him.

The Lord is my Deliverer. He causes me to escape every assault and attack from the enemy. I am delivered from the plague in the name of Jesus Christ my Lord.

The Lord is my God. I have no other God but Jehovah God. The government is not my God. My God is Supreme and Superior to all. His judgment nullifies all others.

The Lord is my Strength. He empowers, energizes and emboldens me to overcome all tests, trials, troubles, tribulations and temptations. I totally depend on the Lord who strengthens me to overcome this month in the name of Jesus Christ my Lord.

The Lord is my Buckler. He shields me from every dart, arrow and plague shot at me. He wards them off from me. That is why no plague touches me.

The Lord is the Horn of my Salvation. He saves me and keeps me safe. I am saved and safe in Christ Jesus my Lord.

The Lord is my High Tower. I am impervious and inaccessible to all plagues and pestilences. No evil shall befall me. I have a vantage position. I am not disadvantaged. I have the advantage because the Lord is my High Tower.

The Lord is my Trust. I am secured, insured and assured because I trust in the Lord Jesus Christ. I am not moved by the government or economy or news. I am moved by God's word that guarantees my security and supplies in the name of Jesus Christ my Lord. Amen.

As you make these confession, watch out for what God is doing. He said that you will SEE His word works. See only His word works. Nothing else. Amen.

I shall not die
I shall not die but live
I shall not die but live to declare the glory of the Lord
You shall not die
They shall not die but live
We shall not die but live to declare the glory of the Lord
In the land of the living, amen.
From SARS-CoV-2 Virus outbreak
From Coronavirus, COVID-19.
I shall not die in Jesus mighty and precious name, amen.
Happy Resurrection!

He is risen! Christ is risen!
Mega blessings!

Author notes : (Dedicated to Aggressive Faith Ministries http://www.aggressivefaith.org. A dedication to Born Again believers in Christ Jesus with faith on Easter Day April 11, 2020 for COVID-19, on SARS-CoV-2 Virus outbreak.)

COVID-19 Jesus Christ Is Lord!

by Funmi Ade-Davies on April 12, 2020. © Mercy Funmilayo Adesanya-Davies, All rights reserved

Jesus Christ is Lord
Jesus Christ is Lord
Jesus Christ is Lord, amen, hallelujah
Every kneel shall bow
Every tongue confess
Jesus Christ is Lord, amen, hallelujah!

Jesus went on a self isolation in the grave for the sin of the world.
He was unduly quarantined though he tested negative to sin.
His Resurrection from His isolation centre after three days formed the foundation for our release from the lock down by sin.
Anyone who has been infected by the virus of sin can be sanitized and recovered through the vaccine of the blood of Jesus.
He will subsequently live a victorious life through the ventilator of the Holy Spirit
Plus he has a mansion home in heaven at last, amen.

Have a blessed Easter season!
Shalom!!!!

Jesus Christ is Lord
Jesus Christ is Lord
Jesus Christ is Lord, amen, hallelujah
Every kneel shall bow
Every tongue confess
Jesus Christ is Lord, amen, hallelujah!

Author notes : (A dedication to the SOURCES on Easter Day 11, April 2020.)

COVID-19: NCDC #TakeResponsibility

by Funmi Ade-Davies on April 12, 2020. © Mercy Funmilayo Adesanya-Davies, All rights reserved

Take Responsibility!
Take Responsibility for COVID
Take Responsibility for COVID-19
Take Responsibility CoV-2
Take Responsibility for SARS-CoV
Take Responsibility for SARS-CoV-2
Take Responsibility!
#TakeResponsibility!

Returning travellers to Nigeria who experience coronavirus symptoms: fever, cough & difficulty breathing should please call NCDC immediately at 080097000010. #TakeResponsibility

Returning travellers to Nigeria: stay home & avoid contact with people including family for 14 days. For NCDC self-isolation guide visit covid19.ncdc.gov.ng #TakeResponsibility!

If you have come in contact with a confirmed coronavirus case & experience fever, cough or difficulty breathing please call NCDC immediately at 080097000010. #TakeResponsibility

Wash your hands frequently with soap under running water. Avoid touching your face & high-contact surfaces to prevent coronavirus spread. #TakeResponsibility!

Prevent coronavirus by cleaning all surfaces frequently. High-contact surfaces include door handles, stair rails and tables. #TakeResponsibility!

Avoid gatherings & physical contact. Practice social distancing by leaving 2 metres distance from others to prevent coronavirus spread. #TakeResponsibility!

Take Responsibility. Coronavirus spreads easily from person to person when people gather together. Stay at home to protect yourself and others. #TakeResponsibility!

Take Responsibility! Stop the spread of fake news. For verified information and regular updates visit covid19.ncdc.gov.ng or @NCDCgov on Facebook and Twitter

#TakeResponsibility!

What are you doing to prevent coronavirus spread in Nigeria? Share on Facebook and
Twitter to join the campaign using the hashtag
#TakeResponsibility!

Take Responsibility!
Take Responsibility for COVID
Take Responsibility for COVID-19
Take Responsibility CoV-2
Take Responsibility for SARS-CoV
Take Responsibility for SARS-CoV-2
Take Responsibility!
#TakeResponsibility!

Of course, yes
Sure, you must take Responsibility
Sure, I must take Responsibility
Certainly, we must take Responsibility
Certainly, they must take Responsibility
Of course, yes
Yes, let us all take Responsibility!

*Author notes : (For COVID-19: From Nigeria Centre for Disease Control (NDCD), Nigeria. Poem
#TakeResponsibility! Dedicated to all obedient Nigerians for Coronavirus campaigns in 2020.)*

COVID-19: Jesus Is Alive!

Jesus is not dead
He's surely alive
He's living on the inside
Living on the inside of me
Am the expression of His image
The expression of his love
Expression of His life
Jesus Christ is alive!

Jesus is no longer in the grave
Jesus is no longer where he laid
He is no longer in the grave
He is alive not dead
I can hear the angels' song
Death could not hold him captive
I can hear the angels say
Let everyone rejoice
Jesus Christ is alive!
Jesus is alive!
Christ is alive!

Jesus is not dead
He's surely alive
He's living on the inside
Living on the inside of me
Am the expression of His image
The expression of his love
Expression of His life
Jesus Christ is alive!

Author notes : (COVID-19: An Easter day dedication to All who believes in Jesus Christ's resurrection power on Easter Day 11 April, 2020)

COVID-19: Plagues and Pandemics

by Funmi Ade-Davies on April 12, 2020. © Mercy Funmilayo Adesanya-Davies, All rights reserved

Pandemics!
Four pandemics!
Are there plagues and pandemics!
Every hundred years?
Four pandemics!
Are there plagues and pandemics!
Pandemics!

Every hundred years?
Every hundred years?
Every hundred years?

1720 — Plague
1820 — Cholera outbreak
1920 — Spanish flu
2020 — Chinese coronavirus.

Great Plague of London, in 1665
The yellow fever, in the late 1800s
The H2N2/Asian flu, in 1957 - 1958
The H3N2 flu virus, in 1968
And the H1N1/swine flu, in 2009
And now SARS-COV-2 Chinesevirus COVID-19,
in 2020.

Pandemics!
Four pandemics!
Are there plagues and pandemics!
Every hundred years?
Four pandemics!
Are there plagues and pandemics!
Pandemics!

Every hundred years?
Every hundred years?
Every hundred years?

COVID-19 AFRICA: There Will Be No Dead Bodies All Over The Streets Of Africa In Jesus Name!

by Funmi Ade-Davies on April 13, 2020. © Mercy Funmilayo Adesanya-Davies, All rights reserved

I see life in Africa
I see light in Africa
I see health in Africa
I see healing in Africa
I see miracles in Africa
I see miracles in Africa
I see recovery in Africa
I do not see dead bodies
I do not see dead bodies all over
I do not see dead bodies all over Africa.

It's not going to be horrible in the developing world!
It is well with All Countries of Africa by the grace of God.
It is well with All Countries of Africa in Jesus precious name.
It is well with All Countries of Africa by the help of the Holy Spirit, Amen.

It is well with Algeria, Angola, Benin, Botswana, Burkina Faso and Burundi
It is well with Cameroon, Cape Verde, Central African Republic, Chad and Camaros
It is well with Democratic Republic of the Congo and Republic of the Congo
It is well with Djibouti, Egypt, Equatorial Guinea Eritrea and Ethiopia
It is well with Gabon, Gambia, Ghana, Guinea and Guinea-Bissau
It is well with Ivory Coast, Kenya, Lesotho, Liberia and Libya
It is well with Madagascar, Malawi, Mali, Mauritania, Mauritius and Morocco
It is well with Mozambique, Namibia, Niger, Nigeria and Rwanda
It is well with Sao Tome and Principe, Senegal, Seychelles and Sierra Leone
It is well with Somalia, South Africa, South Sudan, Sudan and Swaziland
It is well with Tanzania, Togo, Tunisia, Uganda, Zambia and Zimbabwe.

It's not going to be horrible in the developing world!
It is well with All Countries of Africa by the grace of God.
It is well with All Countries of Africa in Jesus precious name.
It is well with All Countries of Africa by the help of the Holy Spirit, Amen.

I am healing
You are healing
We are healing
They are healing
Africa is Healing
Nigeria is healing
The world is healing
We are all recovering
We all are happy and healthy
The earth is becoming better place to live.
In Jesus Christ precious name, Amen.

Author notes : (A dedication to April,13 2020: Today, the full moon begins. According to Jewish belief, it is time to heal. Pray in Jesus name. Segulot (spiritual medicine in Hebrew), only 28 words: "God, our Heavenly Father and our creator, please, come through my house and take all my worries and all my illnesses and, please, come definitively heal my family." Amen. Inspired: God bless Mama Melinda Gates)

COVID-19 And Letter C In This Century!!!

by Funmi Ade-Davies on April 13, 2020. © Mercy Funmilayo Adesanya-Davies, All rights reserved

73

Called (C)
The Corona (C)
It is Coronavirus (C)
Named CoV-2 (C)
Coronavirus 2 (SARS-CoV-2)
Novel Coronavirus (2019-nCoV)
Nick named COVID-19 (C)
It's a medical Case (C)
If person is Confirmed (C)
Needs Confinement (C)
Because of further Contamination (C)
And the entire place need Curfew (C)
Not to lead to the Cemetery (C)
The possible drug is Chloroquine (C)
While it originated from China (C)
It came through the Chinese (C)
By virtue of Conspiracy (C)
Victims need so much Care (C)
The Vaccine takes Commitment (C)
But the real Cure is CHRIST (C)
Please Come (C) unto Jesus!
Let's Champion(C)
This Campaign (C)
And Crusade (C)
Cruise (C)!

Author notes : (A dedication to today 13th. April, 2020 AD and to the 13 Nigerians who died in diaspora listed.)

COVID-19: When we finally....

by Funmi Ade-Davies on April 14, 2020. © Mercy Funmilayo Adesanya-Davies, All rights reserved

When we are all gone
The Art remained
When we've all left
The Books remained.

When we are all gone
The Drawing remained
When we've all left
The Pictures remained.

It all remained the hard
And soft copies ONLY.

When we are all gone
The Painting remained
When we've all left
The Video remained.

When we are all gone

The Account remained
When we've all left
The E-version remained.

It all remained the hard
And soft copies ONLY.

So do your best
And leave the rest
Yesterday is gone
Tomorrow is another day

But today is here.

So do your best
And leave the rest
As it would all remained the hard
And soft copies ONLY.

Author notes : (COVID-19: A
dedication to ALL those who love to read and write.)

COVID-19: An Easter Day Prayer Letter!

by Funmi Ade-Davies on April 14, 2020. © *Mercy Funmilayo Adesanya-Davies, All rights reserved*

Beloved Peace Advocates and families:

Today the power that raised Jesus from the dead is hereby activated in our lives in the name of Jesus.

I see us walking out of this lockdown unscratched. Death could not hold Jesus captive, so no power or situation can hold us captive.

Very soon, I see us dancing and rejoicing because the atmosphere is charged, and rules and protocols are being changed right now for our sake. It is our testimony time in Jesus name.

The voice of the LORD will stand out for us, no matter the noise around our lives. His word will speak for us, no matter what the enemy is saying. We will surely be blessed by the most high God in the name of Jesus.

The LORD will help, keep, uphold, sustain, protect, defend and exalt us in all areas. We will not miss the best of the land, in Jesus mighty name we pray, Amen.

HE IS RISEN!
HAPPY EASTER!!
STAY SAFE!!!

Author notes : (For: POLAC PEACE ADVOCATES Amb. Sir & Dame Mike Jukwe, KSS, KofC, Amb. P. Country President: Easter day prayer, 12th April 2020)

Covid -19: Case File

77

Case is closed
With Christ' resurrection
Where's death sting!

Author notes : (COVID -19 CORONAVIRUS: Dedicated to all the dead in Christ on Easter Monday 13th April 2020: 13 WORDS: Christ Has Won The Victory!)

Faith In Times Of COVID-19

Whosoever shall lose his life shall gain it
Whosoever shall gain his life shall lose it
Says Jesus Christ our Lord said!

Faith is simple
if you loose
it's time to gain.

"simplicity is complex
if you want nothing
you have everything."

"a winter's evening
tattooed with stars-
warmth of a fire."

A day in rains
drawn in water's pull
dried with no sun.

Whosoever shall lose his life shall gain it
Whosoever shall gain his life shall lose it
Says Jesus Christ our Lord!

Author notes : (COVID-19: A dedication to ALL still in FAITH against Coronavirus on 2020 Easter day.)

COVID-19: Christ Has Won The Victory!

COVID-19
Coronavirus, SAR-CoV-2
Christ Has Won The Victory!
Christ is risen! He is risen!
Tell it out with joyful voice.
He has burst his three days' prison;
Let the whole wide earth rejoice.
Death is conquered; man is free.
Christ has won the victory.
Christ Has Won The Victory!

COVID-19
Coronavirus, SAR-CoV-2
Christ Has Won The Victory!
Come with high and holy hymning;
Chant our Lord's triumphant lay.
Not one darksome cloud is dimming
Yonder glorious morning ray,
Breaking o'er the purple east,
Symbol of our Easter feast.
Christ Has Won The Victory!

COVID-19
Coronavirus, SAR-CoV-2
Christ Has Won The Victory!
He is risen! He is risen!
He hath opened heaven's gate.
We are free from sin's dark prison,
Risen to a holier state.
And a brighter Easter beam
On our longing eyes shall stream.
Christ Has Won The Victory!

Author notes : (Dedicated to: Writers Cecil Frances Alexander, 1818–1895. Music: Joachim Neander, 1650–1680. EASTER Hymn on Easter day April 12, 2020)

Covid-19 Sars-Cov-2: God is Ultimate!

I want to know
In the heat of the COVID-19 outbreak
You want to know
In the heat of the Coronavirus pandemic
They want to know
In the heat of SARS-CoV-2 Virus outbreak
We all want to know
In the heat of the novel coronavirus
What is the ultimate
GOD is Ultimate!

God made the sun
God made the moon
God made the stars
God made the earth
God made the water
God made the wind
God made the rain
God made the planets
And this universe
God made them all!

I want to know (everybody wants to know)
I want to know (everybody wants to know)
I want to know (everybody wants to know)
Oh, I want to know (everybody wants to know)?

I know man made the trains
Man made the planes
Man made the guns
Man made the bombs
Man made the ships
Man made the cars
God made the man
God made the woman
God made them all!

I want to know (everybody wants to know)
I want to know (everybody wants to know)
I want to know (everybody wants to know)
Oh, I want to know (everybody wants to know)!

I heard a voice in the wilderness
Saying God made them all
God made man in His own likeness
God is not man, let God be God
God made the plants
God made the beasts
God made the flowers
God made the trees
God made the darkness
God made the light
God made them all!

Yeah, now I know(everybody wants to know)
Yeah, now you know (everybody wants to know)
Yeah, now we know (everybody wants to know)
Yeah, now they know (everybody wants to know)!

Yeah, now I know, God made them all
The birds, fish and the flowers
The trees, the sun and moon
The stars, the earth, planets, and all the universe...
God made them all!

I want to know
In the heat of the COVID-19 outbreak
You want to know
In the heat of the Coronavirus pandemic
They want to know
In the heat of SARS-CoV-2 Virus outbreak
We all want to know
In the heat of the novel coronavirus
What is the ultimate
GOD is Ultimate!

But who made the laws?
What's wrong and right?
Who made them right and wrong?
The voice in the wilderness...

82

Author notes : (DEDICATED To The Source: Musixmatch, the Songwriters Jimmy Cliff: I Want to Know lyrics; and © Ppx Publishing (bmi), Songs Supreme Ltd. So inspiring in this season !)

COVID-19: Respect, We Need Each Other!

by Funmi Ade-Davies on April 14, 2020. © Mercy Funmilayo Adesanya-Davies, All rights reserved

We'd all shared good and bad times together
But now in this our times of most need and distress
Why can we not find you to help us again
Why can't we share this time together
Let's give ourselves a chance
Let's give ourselves the chance
Let's give ourselves one more chance
Let's give the creation a chance
Let's give the world a chance!

Respect, you need me
I need you
Respect, we need you
You need us
We all need one another
To fight to cnd this Coronavirus
As one people and body!

China is suddenly recovering
America is seriously lamenting
Italians are massively dying
Spaniards are deeply crying
Africans are getting the heat
Nigerians are trying hard!

We'd all shared good and bad times together as nations
But now in this our times of most need and distress as a globe
Why can we not find you to help us again as one world
Why can't we share this time together as one creation
Let's give ourselves as nations a chance!
Let's give ourselves as the globe the chance
Let's give our world one more chance
Let's give the creation a chance
Let's give the world a chance!

Respect, you need me
I need you
Respect, we need you
You need us
We all need one another
To fight to end this Coronavirus
As one single planet earth!

Author notes : (Dedicated to us and our planet earth on 2020 EASTER DAY CELEBRATIONS!!!)

COVID-19 Palliatives!

85

COVID-19 Palliatives
COVID-19 Palliatives in Nigeria
COVID-19 Palliative in Africa!

You share COVID -19 palliatives
As if you're COVID immune
Are you COVID immune?
You are stealing and looting
You are enjoying the looting
Of Mr. COVID-19 palliatives
As if you're COVID immune
Are you immune at all?
At all, are you immune?
As if you're God Himself!

You share COVID -19 palliatives:
To your family and friends
To your relations and acquaintances
To your neighbours and colleagues
To your hamlets and villages
To your LGA and zones
To your townsmen and statesmen
And not to Nigeria as a nation
And not to Nigerians as people
As if you're God Himself!

You share COVID-19 palliatives
As if you're COVID immune
Are you COVID immune?
You are relaxing and resting
You are enjoying the stealing
Of Mr. Coronavirus palliatives
As if you're COVID immune
Are you immune to it?
To it, are you immune?
As if you're God Himself!

COVID-19 Palliatives
COVID-19 Palliatives in Nigeria
COVID-19 Palliatives in Africa!

This palliative is just an action everywhere
Intended to cushen the effects somehow
Of coronavirus and make it less severe
Not actually to solve the problem whatever
Neither is it a political sharing whichever
To tidy all your ends anyhow!

Author notes : (Dedicated to all those who were not given any palliatives during the Coronavirus COVID-19 pandemic outbreak lockdown.)

Printed by Books on Demand GmbH, Norderstedt / Germany